Backyard Birds
of Summer

CAROL LERNER

Morrow Junior Books • *New York*

For Ralph

The author thanks Charles Nelson,
director of the Sarett Nature Center in
Benton Harbor, Michigan, for
reviewing the manuscript.

Watercolors were used for the full-color illustrations.
The text type is 13.5-point Caslon 540.

Printed in Hong Kong by South China Printing Company (1988) Ltd.

1 2 3 4 5 6 7 8 9 10

Library of Congress Cataloging-in-Publication Data
Lerner, Carol.
Backyard birds of summer/Carol Lerner.
p. cm.
Includes bibliographical references and index.
Summary: Describes primarily those species of birds that are
tropical migrants visiting the North only during the nesting season.
Includes suggestions for attracting birds to one's yard.
ISBN 0-688-13600-1 (trade)—ISBN 0-688-13601-X (library)
1. Birds—North America—Juvenile literature.
2. Birds—Summering—North America—Juvenile literature.
3. Bird attracting—North America—Juvenile literature.
[1. Birds—Attracting.   2. Birds—Habits and behavior.]
I. Title.   QL681.L43 1996   598.297—dc20   95-12652   CIP   AC

CONTENTS

INTRODUCTION: BIRDS IN SUMMER

Spring is a restless time for all birds. Some winter residents are taking flight, headed for far northern nesting grounds. Birds that moved to the southern states to spend the cold months are returning to their summer homes. Even the birds that live year-round in the same place are in movement, as they stake out territory for the nesting season.

The most dramatic change is the arrival of summer visitors from the tropical regions of the Americas. Each year, as the sun moves to the northern latitudes, waves of colorful birds come from the forests and mountains of Mexico, the West Indies, and Central and South America. They remain in their summer homes for a few short months while they nest and raise their young.

In summer, as in other seasons, most birds seen in backyards and neighborhoods are likely to be the year-round residents—chickadees and titmice, woodpeckers and finches—that live their entire life cycle on the same grounds. This book focuses on the rarer summer visitors that brighten their ranks each year.

The majority of the species described here are tropical migrants that visit the North only during the nesting season. Others are birds that winter in the deep South or near the coasts of the United States but then move northward when spring comes.

More and more people who began by feeding birds in winter now leave their feeders up all year. In spring and summer they can expect to see some visitors from the South and from the far tropics among the more familiar backyard birds. They also assure themselves of a front-row seat as all birds play out the dramas of these seasons: some species going through elaborate rituals of threat and bluff as they compete for space and set up boundaries for their territories; some engaging in courtship displays at the feeders as they pair off and prepare to mate. Later, after the young have left the nest, backyard birders can watch as troops of half-grown offspring trail their parents on visits to the yard.

A rich variety of foods is available to birds in the growing season: insects, spiders, worms, buds, flowers, and fruits. The birds take full advantage of these foods, and almost all species—even the seed-eaters—feed their young on high-protein animal food.

In spite of this banquet, feeding stations provide a welcome supplement. Spring and summer are the most stressful months in the birds' yearly cycle. The adults spend enormous amounts of energy while defending their territories and nests, laying eggs, and bringing food to their helpless nestlings. Then, after their young are raised, adult birds undergo their annual molt as old feathers drop out and new ones replace them. And finally, as summer ends, the birds that will be migrating must put on extra layers of fat to fuel their long flights. During each of these periods the birds require extra food.

In hot, dry areas where ponds and streams are scarce, providing a supply of water may be even more helpful than a well-stocked feeder. Birds cannot sweat, but when their bodies are in danger of overheating, they cool off just as dogs do, by panting. As birds breathe through their open mouths, moisture evaporates from their tissues and this cools their bodies. The lost water needs to be replaced, of course, either by eating moist food or by drinking. Apart from that, birds also enjoy water for bathing, especially in hot weather.

While summer feeding stations can help relieve the demands of the season, some birds are threatened by a more serious and permanent danger. Loss of habitat in both the Southern and Northern Hemispheres casts a shadow over the future of numerous species.

Many of our songbirds have decreased in population over the last half century. Those that migrate from the American tropics have been especially hard hit because of the large-scale destruction of Latin American forests in recent decades. As more and more of these forests are burned and bulldozed to become farms and grazing fields, the birds that winter there are left homeless. Open fields offer no shelter for woodland birds.

This destruction of forests does little to solve the long-term problem of human hunger in Latin America, because the soils of those lush tropical forests have very low fertility. After only a few years of cultivation, most new fields become worthless for agriculture and are abandoned.

But as long as the human population in these regions continues its rapid growth, the pressure to turn forest into farm will also continue, and the birds will suffer further loss of habitat.

Tropical birds arriving at their northern nesting areas often find that these habitats too have eroded. The great forests that once covered most of the eastern United States are long gone, of course. But what is left continues to be lost to housing and other developments, to road building, and to logging. With each clearing, the remnants of woodland are divided into ever-smaller pieces. As a result, there is less safety for the birds nesting within them.

Outside predators—dogs, cats, rats, gray squirrels, and raccoons—all find it easier to raid nests that are built near the edges of forests. The same is true of birds that prey on the eggs and nestlings of other birds. Jays, crows, and grackles are nest robbers, and they are more numerous on the margins of woodlands than in the interior.

But the greatest danger is from cowbirds, which take the highest toll on the young of other bird species. The brown-headed cowbird and its relative in the Southwest, the bronzed cowbird, are the only North American birds that make no nests for their eggs. Instead, a female cowbird watches as other birds build their nests. When she discovers a finished nest, the cowbird often removes some of the eggs she finds there by pushing them over the edge. Then, having made room, she lays her own eggs and flies off, leaving them for the other bird to raise. Strangely enough, the host birds often accept the cowbird eggs and, after they hatch, treat the foreign nestlings as their own offspring.

Cowbirds are birds of open fields and seldom wander into deep forests. Before the eastern forests of the United States were cleared, most cowbirds probably lived in the prairies west of the Mississippi. The removal of the great woodlands created an opportunity for them to extend their range eastward. As forests continue to be broken into smaller and smaller fragments, more forest nests come within the cowbirds' reach.

Birds that nest in tree holes have also suffered from changes in the North American forests. Woodpeckers and some other species dig nest holes in dead or infected trees. Many other kinds of birds depend upon finding ready-made holes—an old woodpecker nest or a tree cavity caused by decay—where they can lay eggs and raise their young.

With less remaining woodland, their chances are fewer. Even where forests still grow, dying trees are often cut from managed woodlots and parklands because they may harbor insect pests and appear unattractive. In towns and suburbs, homeowners remove such trees from their properties, regarding them as ugly or dangerous.

Still another threat comes from two alien species that compete with native birds for the remaining nest holes. European starlings and house sparrows were brought to North America in the nineteenth century, and their flocks quickly spread from coast to coast. Since they live in the same place year-round, these introduced birds get first pick of the best nest sites. They are already nesting before the migrators arrive.

Birdhouses and nesting boxes can replace some of the lost nesting sites. A number of hole-nesting birds have become accustomed to these substitute homes, and several species now depend upon them. Some birds have adapted to the housing shortage by nesting in the crannies of buildings, bridges, and other structures.

Anyone who has a yard can provide a bit of sanctuary for these hard-pressed summer visitors. Of course, there is no guarantee that the birds described in this book will land in your backyard. The likelihood is greater if you live near some kind of attractive habitat—parkland, forest, open fields, or a body of water. But with offerings of food, water, and shelter, even a small yard may become a welcome refuge for all birds.

The last chapter gives information about food, birdbaths, feeders, and birdhouses and suggests ways to make your yard more inviting to birds.

The summer birds in the first section of the book are species that can be attracted to yards by an offering of food and water. The second section describes birds that will use nesting boxes. Most of the birds in this second section feed only on insects and will not come to feeding stations to eat. A few of the birds included—bluebirds and the Bewick's wren—are present in much of their range year-round. But it is only during the nesting season, of course, that they can be lured to birdhouses.

The illustrations show adult birds as they appear in the mating season. Birds are shown in approximate actual size, and a map for each species shows its summer range.

FEEDER BIRDS

Grosbeaks

The finches are a large bird family that is found in almost every part of the world. Finches are seed-eaters that have strong cone-shaped beaks for cracking the hard shells of their food.

Even among finches, grosbeaks ("large beaks") stand out because of their unusually large bills. Although their bills are designed for seed-eating, finches like a variety of foods. They also eat insects—especially during the nesting season—and fruits.

The male rose-breasted grosbeak is a startling sight at the feeder. He is large, with a massive pale bill. He has bold black-and-white markings and a brilliant rose red bib. When he flies, you may be able to see another patch of red under each wing. His mate has the same heavy bill but none of his color. She is dark brown above with brown streaks on her pale breast and sides.

The pair nests in a tree or bush near an open field. Cowbirds often discover the nest and deposit eggs in it.

ROSE-BREASTED
GROSBEAK

The grosbeak likes sunflower seeds at feeders. It is also attracted to gardens with flowering trees and shrubs. It eats the buds, blossoms, fruits, and seeds and searches through the branches for insects. The bird has earned the name potato-bug bird because it often feeds on the destructive Colorado potato beetle.

The rose-breasted grosbeak winters between Mexico and the northern part of South America.

The black-headed grosbeak is the western version of the rose-breasted. The two species are closely related and similar in everything but the color of their feathers. They have the same huge beak, the same eating habits in the wild and at feeders, and they are at home in similar habitats. On the Great Plains, where their ranges meet, the two species sometimes mate.

The male black-headed has rust-colored underparts and, of course, a black head. The female is similar to the female rose-breasted except that her unmarked breast is light brown, and she has less streaking on her sides.

Black-headed grosbeaks fly to Mexico for the winter.

BLACK-HEADED GROSBEAK

In summer the blue grosbeak is found nearly coast to coast in the United States except in the North. It nests in trees or bushes in open areas—old fields, bushy borders along roads or fences, overgrown gardens. The nests often suffer from use by cowbirds.

The blue grosbeak is a little smaller than the other North American grosbeaks but has the same big bill. Like them, it feeds on seeds, insects, and fruit and prefers sunflower seeds at feeders. It also takes corn and wheat from farmers' fields.

The male is deep blue and has two rust-colored bars on each wing. In poor light the bird appears to be black. The female is brown with tan wing bars.

You might be able to identify this bird by its behavior. When perched, it has a habit of twitching its tail and spreading its tail feathers wide open and then closing them.

Blue grosbeaks migrate to spend winter between Mexico and Panama. Some fly to the Caribbean Islands.

BLUE GROSBEAK

Buntings

These too are finches. But buntings are smaller than grosbeaks, and their bills are much more delicate.

INDIGO BUNTING

The indigo bunting is a bird of woodland edges and overgrown fields. Over the last century, as farms and pastures were deserted and many woodlands were cut, the amount of habitat for this species has increased. Formerly an eastern bird, it now nests in some of the southwestern states. The nest is built a few feet above the ground in a low tree or bushy thicket, where it is often found by cowbirds.

The male indigo sings all summer long, keeping watch over his territory from a nearby perch and warning other birds away. In the sunlight he is a brilliant blue. In shadow, or with the light behind him, he may look black. The female is plain brown.

Indigos eat large numbers of insects, along with seeds and small fruits. At feeders, they like small seeds such as niger (NI-jer) and millet.

They winter in Mexico, Central America, and the West Indies.

In the West, the lazuli (LAZZ-you-lee) bunting takes the place of the indigo. Where their ranges overlap, the two sometimes mate and produce mixed young, but they are still considered to be separate species.

Lazuli buntings eat the same kinds of food as indigos and are alike in their habits and habitat. As more western forests are cut, more areas become available to them. The development of farm irrigation systems with growths of thickets along their banks has also increased the buntings' habitat.

The male lazuli bunting is bright blue, with cinnamon on the breast and sides and white wing bars. The female also has wing bars, but otherwise she resembles the female indigo bunting.

A few lazuli buntings winter in southern Arizona and New Mexico, but most fly to Mexico.

LAZULI BUNTING

PAINTED BUNTING

Male painted buntings are a rainbow of red, blue, green, and purple. Until they came under the protection of federal law, males were sold as cage birds in the United States.

Females are greenish above and yellow-green below.

The painted bunting is a shy bird. It lurks in shrubs and brush piles, searching for seeds and insects on the ground. It comes to southern feeders to eat sunflower and niger seeds, as well as mixed birdseed.

Most buntings fly to Cuba, the Bahamas, Mexico, and Central America for the winter. A few remain in Florida and along the Gulf Coast.

Gray Catbird

The mimics *(Mimidae)* are a family of Western Hemisphere birds with the ability to imitate the sounds they hear around them. The gray catbird is one of these mimics. One catbird was heard giving the calls of forty different species of birds. Other catbirds imitate frogs or the spitting sound made by cats.

The catbird is named for its own distinctive call, which is a catlike *mew*. Males and females look alike. They are plain gray with black caps and long black tails. The only color is a patch of rusty brown beneath the tail.

The birds are at home in thickets. They nest in hedges, in weedy overgrown corners of gardens, or in bushes at the woodland's edge. Although they eat great numbers of insects, they have a passion for small fruits. Raisins softened in water will lure them to feeders. If your yard has berry bushes, the birds are likely to show up. But if you want to save the berries for yourself, you will have to find a way to outwit the catbirds.

Catbirds migrate in fall. Most fly to Mexico, Central America, or the West Indies. Part of the population remains in coastal areas of the southern and southeastern United States.

GRAY CATBIRD

Hummingbirds

This is a large family with over three hundred and forty species, and it is found only in the Western Hemisphere. The greatest number of species live near the equator in South America. Eight kinds are commonly seen in some parts of the United States, and four of these also nest in Canada.

Everything about hummingbirds is special: their small size, glittering feathers, and acrobatic movements in the air. Their brightest colors—the blazing reds and blues on throats and crowns—come from light reflecting off their feathers. These flashing colors are visible only when the bird is directly before you. From other angles the same area will look green or black.

As in almost all species of birds, male hummingbirds have the brightest feathers. Females generally lack the colorful throat markings. In fact, females of the North American species are so much alike that it is often impossible to identify them with certainty.

Hummingbirds can fly in all directions—up, down, backward, sideways—and upside down. They feed in the air, hovering in place before tube-shaped flowers. To collect enough food, hummingbirds must visit two thousand to five thousand flowers each day. They slip their thin bills into the blossom and lick up the nectar with long tongues. Small insects and spiders from the flower also become part of their diet.

The females make their nests in trees, bushes, vines, or—in the case of desert species—cactus plants.

Hummingbirds are attracted to yards by many kinds of flowers and by sugar water in hummingbird feeders.

RUBY-THROATED
HUMMINGBIRD

The ruby-throated hummingbird is the only species that lives in eastern North America. In the spring, it arrives in the northern parts of its range before many of its food plants are in flower. In these early weeks, the hummingbird may depend on tree sap rather than flower nectar for food. Woodpeckers known as sapsuckers drill holes in tender tree bark and then drink the sap that oozes out. Hummingbirds follow sapsuckers and feed at the same holes.

The rubythroat winters from Mexico to Costa Rica.

17

Anna's hummingbird lives year-round in most of its range, and it is the most common hummingbird in California. It is found in bushy thickets and also in wooded groves, orchards, and gardens. Until the middle years of the 1960s, it was seldom seen in states other than California. Since then, Anna's has expanded north, south, and east. The cause is uncertain, but it may be loss of habitat in California. Another possible reason is the increase in suburban gardens, making food plants more widely available. A third possibility is that the population of Anna's may be growing, forcing young birds to seek new territories.

The male Anna's has a head and throat of rosy red. The female usually has some streaks or patches of red on her throat too.

Costa's hummingbird nests in desert areas. After the spring nesting season, it moves to the same kind of shrubby habitat where Anna's hummingbird often lives. You can recognize the Costa male by his dark violet crown and throat and the long violet feathers that extend down the sides of his neck.

Some Costa's hummingbirds stay in southern California and southwestern Arizona all year, while others migrate to Mexico.

Allen's hummingbird usually nests in woodland areas, but it is a frequent visitor to gardens along the California coast.

The throat of the male is orange-red; his cheeks, sides, and tail are reddish brown. He is green on his back and the top of his head.

Most Allen's hummingbirds migrate to Mexico for winter. Some colonies live year-round on the Channel Islands, off the southern coast of California.

ANNA'S
HUMMINGBIRD

COSTA'S
HUMMINGBIRD

ALLEN'S
HUMMINGBIRD

The rufous hummingbird is the most northern member of the family. It nests from northern California to southern Alaska. In its long migration to and from Mexico, the rufous travels through most of the West, from the Pacific coast to the Rocky Mountains.

Like the ruby-throated hummingbird, the rufous takes advantage of sapsucker holes to feed on tree sap.

The male has an orange-red throat and reddish sides and tail. It is the only North American hummingbird with a reddish brown back.

The three-inch caliope (cal-EYE-oh-pee) hummingbird is the smallest bird found north of Mexico. Females often nest high in the western mountains, all the way from California up to British Columbia and Alberta in Canada. Nighttime temperatures in these mountains may reach freezing, but in spite of their small size (one-tenth of an ounce), the females are able to produce enough body heat to keep the young warm.

The male has a white throat marked with streaks of dark purple.

Like the rufous hummingbird, the caliope is seen over a wide area during spring and fall migration. Its winter home is in Mexico.

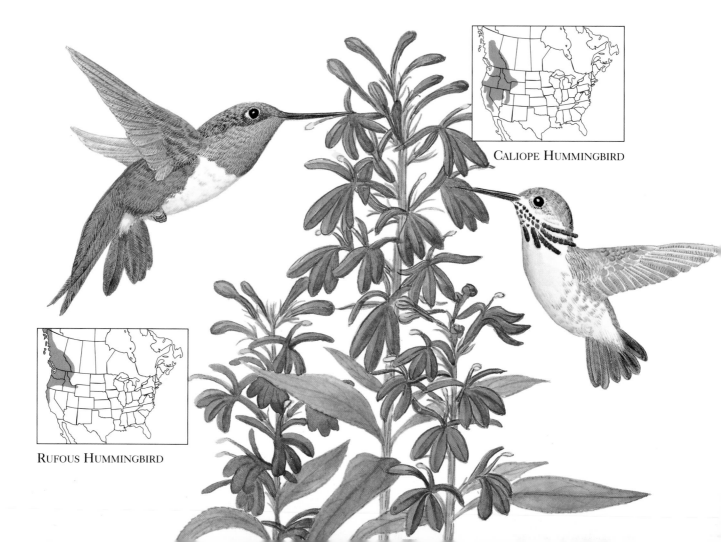

CALIOPE HUMMINGBIRD

RUFOUS HUMMINGBIRD

The broad-tailed hummingbird also nests in mountain ranges. It is common in the Rockies and in the mountains of the Great Basin.

The male's wings make a loud whistling sound when he flies. In his coloring, he looks like a male ruby-throated hummingbird, but the rubythroat is not found this far west.

The broad-tailed spends winter in Mexico and Central America.

Black-chinned hummingbirds are closely related to the eastern ruby-throat. While males of other species may appear to have black throats when they are seen in poor light, this is the only male with a truly black chin. In good light, you can see a band of violet that borders the lower part of the throat.

It is a common species in the West, where it nests over a very wide area. Most black-chins winter in Mexico.

BROAD-TAILED
HUMMINGBIRD

BLACK-CHINNED
HUMMINGBIRD

Orioles

Orioles have such brilliant colors and beautiful songs that it is hard to think of them as relatives of blackbirds and cowbirds. But all these birds belong to the same family—the troupials—a family found only in the Americas.

Orioles are famous for building elaborate nests. They start by hanging loops of plant fibers from the tip of a tree branch. Then they weave grass and other plants in and out through the loops to make a hanging basket. Finally, they line the inside with hair or feathers.

In the wild, orioles feed on insects and berries. They also like to eat the sweet nectar found in flowers, the same nectar that attracts bees and other insects. They reach the nectar at the base of long tube-shaped flowers by pecking a hole at the bottom of the tube.

Orioles visit hummingbird feeders in order to feed their sweet tooth. They are also attracted to fruits at feeding stations—grapes, watermelon, orange halves—and to peanut butter mixtures and suet.

BALTIMORE ORIOLE

BULLOCK'S ORIOLE

The Baltimore oriole is seen across southern Canada and the eastern United States. The male has a bright orange rump and underparts, a black hood, and a narrow band of white on his black wings. The female is olive brown above with dull orange underparts.

A similar bird, Bullock's oriole, summers in the West. The male of this species shows the same orange, black, and white colors as the Baltimore, but his face is orange with a black eye streak and each wing has a large patch of white. His mate is much like the female Baltimore but with yellow beneath the chin and a white belly.

In 1973 scientists decided to consider these two orioles as one: the northern oriole. But in 1995 they reversed the decision and separated the birds once again into two species, Baltimore and Bullock's.

Both species nest along woodland edges and country roads, and in shade trees of towns and backyards. They migrate to Mexico and Central America in fall. Recently, more and more orioles have stayed through the winter in California or in coastal areas of the southeastern United States, Louisiana, and Texas.

ORCHARD ORIOLE

As the name suggests, orchard orioles often nest in fruit trees, whether in orchards or around homes. They also use shade trees in parks, gardens, fields, or along streets.

These birds are often victims of cowbirds. This is especially true in the Rio Grande Valley of Texas, where many become unwilling foster parents to young bronzed cowbirds. The orchard oriole population has fallen, especially in the western part of their range.

Males have a brick red breast and a black hood, wings, and tail. Females are a dull yellow and olive.

After the young are raised, these orioles leave for their winter homes in Mexico, Central America, and South America.

SCOTT'S ORIOLE

Scott's oriole flies north from Mexico to spend the nesting season in arid regions of the southwestern United States. Yucca plants are favorite nesting places, along with Joshua trees, palms, and piñon pines.

Males are bright lemon yellow and black. Females are dull green-yellow with streaked backs. As the females age, their throats show some black markings.

As a side effect of some human activities, hooded orioles have been expanding their range in the United States. Plantings of palm trees and of gardens with nectar-rich flowers have encouraged them to spread northward in California. And hummingbird feeders have attracted increasing numbers to southwestern cities.

The nests of hooded orioles are often used by bronzed cowbirds.

Males have orange hoods and a black patch from the eyes to the throat. Females have a dull olive-and-yellow coloring similar to that of females of other oriole species.

In fall most hooded orioles return to Mexico for the winter.

HOODED ORIOLE

Tanagers

The tanagers (TAN-ih-jurs) are a family of birds living in the dense forests of tropical America. Scientists have described over two hundred and forty different kinds and are still discovering new species in the high mountains of the Andes. Even though many tanagers are brightly colored, the birds are not easy to see, for they spend their lives hidden in treetops or deep thickets.

You can tell the colorful tanagers and orioles apart by their beaks: Tanager bills are heavier and shaped like a cone, while oriole bills are long and sharply pointed.

Only a few kinds of tanagers leave their tropical homelands, but four species fly northward each spring to mate and raise their young in the woodlands of the United States and Canada. They feed heavily on insects, picking them off branches and leaves or snatching them in mid-air.

Like most tanagers, these visiting species also eat fruit. Sometimes they stop at feeders for oranges, bananas, or grapes, or for raisins that have been softened in water. They also like soft bread crumbs and peanut butter mixtures.

One of the visiting tanager species—the hepatic—is seen only in the southwestern corner of the United States, but the other three are found over very widespread areas.

SCARLET TANAGER

Most scarlet tanagers migrate from South American forests east of the Andes Mountains. In spring you can hear the males singing from high branches in the forest. Some pairs raise their young close to people, nesting in large shade trees in parks and suburban yards.

After the nesting season, the male will lose his red head and body covering as new feathers of yellow-green grow in. Until the molt is complete, his body will be a patchwork of red and yellow. When it's over, he will look like his olive green mate except that his wings and tail will be a darker black.

The summer tanager is a common summer bird in parts of the South, though it has been disappearing from the eastern part of its range. It settles down in woodlands or in more open areas, sometimes nesting in trees that are close to houses. Southerners call it the red bee-bird because it is often seen catching bees and wasps from the air. The bird sometimes hovers around the eaves of houses, looking for insects or spiders.

Males are rosy red all over and keep the same color throughout the year. Females look much like a female scarlet tanager, but their wings are not as dark, and they may show a hint of orange in their yellow breast and belly feathers.

During our fall and winter, summer tanagers may live anywhere from central Mexico to the Amazon River of Brazil.

SUMMER TANAGER

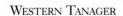

WESTERN TANAGER

Western tanagers come from the highlands of Mexico and Central America to nest in the evergreen forests of the West.

In spring the male is the most colorful of all the visiting tanagers, but his red head changes to yellow-green in the fall. Both the male and female can be told apart from the other yellowish tanagers by the bands of white or yellow seen on their folded wings.

BIRDS USING HOUSES

Wrens

Wrens are quick, busy birds with upturned tails. Most are small, brown or brown-gray in color, and rather secretive. Living close to the ground, they move through bushes and other low plants, picking up insects in their thin, sharp bills. Males and females look alike.

The Western Hemisphere is home to the wren family. The largest number of species live in Central and South America, but ten are found in North America, and one—known as the winter wren—has spread to Europe and Asia.

The house wren is the most widespread of the North American wrens and the most common wren in the East. It feeds on insects and spiders and does not visit feeders, but of all the backyard-nesting birds, it is the easiest to attract to a bird box. The female is fussy about where she nests. Even if a house is waiting, she may prefer a woodpile or a tangle of bushes. Some choose very strange places: an old shoe, a mailbox or empty tin can, a flowerpot, the pocket of a pair of pants on a clothesline. One wren built her nest in the felt hat worn by a scarecrow.

House wrens are not shy during the nesting season, and they make a lot of noise for their size. The song is a string of bubbly notes, delivered from perches all around the yard. The male begins singing when he arrives in spring and continues while the young are growing up.

House wrens are the plainest wrens, with no sharp, clear markings. They have fine black stripes on their wings, sides, and tail, but you can see these only with binoculars or when the bird is very close.

In fall the house wren migrates to the southern edges of the United States or down into Mexico.

HOUSE WREN

BEWICK'S WREN

The population of Bewick's (BUE-icks) wrens has fallen sharply in the East. In the western part of its range, it is more numerous than the house wren and replaces it as a common backyard bird. The two species are alike in their nesting habits and insect diet. But, unlike the house wren, Bewick's wren is a year-round bird in most of the areas where it nests.

Bewick's wren is a little larger than the house wren, with a white stripe over each eye and white underparts. Its tail is longer, rounded at the end, and edged with white spots.

31

Swallows

Birds in the worldwide swallow family live entirely on insects caught in the air. These streamlined birds speed through the sky on long pointed wings, scooping insects into their open mouths. They even manage to drink and take a bath on the wing by dipping into the water as they skim over lakes and ponds.

They are graceful in the air but clumsy on land. Their legs are short and their feet small and weak, making it difficult for them to walk. To rest, they often perch on telephone or electric wires or on bare branches. When they sit above you, you can see the forked tails that are characteristic of many swallow species.

Most swallows that nest in the United States and Canada come from Central and South America. During their stay in the North, they catch huge numbers of insects for food, so they need broad open areas where they can chase down their prey. They also need a hole or some other cranny that will hold a nest. Many swallows now use birdhouses or some kind of human structure as a nest site. If they succeed in raising a brood of young, the birds are likely to return to the same nesting place next spring.

In the wild, purple martins make their homes in a tree hole, an old woodpecker nest, or some other natural cavity. Usually a single pair nests by itself.

Over the centuries, people have tried to attract these birds, hoping that the martins would clear the air of mosquitoes and other flying insects. The Native Americans raised hollow gourds on poles to serve as martin homes. The birds soon learned to accept people as neighbors and to use houses with many separate apartments. Most eastern birds now use martin houses. In the West, many still nest in natural holes.

Martins are the largest North American swallows. Males are shiny purple-blue but look black against the sky. Females are grayish blue above and pale below. This difference is unusual in the swallow family, where males and females of most species look the same.

Like other swallows, martins eat only insects and are not attracted by the usual feeder foods. However, they may come to feeding areas to pick up bits of eggshell scattered on the ground.

PURPLE MARTIN

33

BARN SWALLOW

TREE SWALLOW

The barn swallow is the most widespread of all the world's swallows. It nests in Europe, Asia, northern Africa, and the Middle East, as well as North America.

Sheds, barns, bridges, and boat docks are its favorite nesting places. Before North America was settled, the swallow may have chosen a rock ledge, a cave, or a tree trunk. Now most use a building or other structure that stands close to open fields or a body of water. A pair makes a deep cup-shaped nest of mud and dry grass plastered on a shelf or ledge.

Barn swallows are shiny blue-black on top with rusty red underparts. Their tails have a deep fork.

Compared to other swallows, the hardy little tree swallow endures much colder weather. It is the first of its family to arrive in the North, appearing in New England before the end of March. On chilly days in early spring, when insects are scarce, tree swallows eat weed seeds and some wild fruits. Most other swallows would starve in the absence of insects.

In winter, tree swallows migrate just far enough south to avoid the worst cold. Some spend winter on the southern edges of the United States, from California to southeastern Virginia; the rest go to Central America and the West Indies. But in mild winters, some stay along the Atlantic coast as far north as Massachusetts and survive by eating bayberries.

Tree swallows compete with starlings and English sparrows for tree holes, but now most use houses that are set out by bird lovers.

These swallows are shiny blue or blue-green above and pure white below.

34

Eastern Phoebe

The eastern phoebe belongs to the largest family in the Western Hemisphere. The family is known as the tyrant flycatchers—*tyrant* because some members are quick to fight, and *flycatcher* because they dart out to snatch flies and other insects from the air. This family lives only in the Western Hemisphere.

Most flycatchers feed entirely on insect food and do not visit feeders. They perch on bare twigs or wires, watching for prey. You can recognize them by their large heads and upright posture as they sit and wait.

The eastern phoebe is an unusually tame bird. Even when nesting, it shows little fear of people. In the wild, a phoebe makes its nest on a rock wall or in a cave, but many now choose bridges, barns or sheds, the eaves of houses, or door- or windowsills. A nesting shelf on the side of a house or garage may attract them.

Their population appears to be falling in parts of the East and Midwest. In part this is because cowbirds so often deposit their eggs in phoebe nests.

The eastern phoebe, like many of its family, is rather plain, with dull brown-gray above and light underparts. The two sexes look alike. One way to recognize the bird is by its tail-wagging habit. A phoebe sitting on a perch jerks its tail up and down. Sometimes it calls its name: a raspy, repeated *fee-bee, fee-bee, fee-bee.*

Some eastern phoebes migrate to Mexico in fall. Others stay in the southern states, from Virginia to the Gulf of Mexico.

EASTERN PHOEBE

35

Bluebirds

The thrush family is a large one. It has over three hundred different species, with members living in almost every part of the world.

Unlike other thrushes, bluebirds nest only in holes—in dead trees or old woodpecker nests. In the eastern United States, where there are fewer and fewer of these natural cavities, the population of bluebirds dropped steeply during the past century. All three species of North American bluebirds will use birdhouses as a substitute for natural holes. Any kind of open area is suitable for a house—a meadow, park, garden, or golf course.

Bluebirds eat insects and some berries and other small fruits. If they live nearby, they might be attracted to feeders by a mixture of peanut butter, fat, and cornmeal. Some people feed them mealworms.

In the warmer parts of the United States, bluebirds remain in the area year-round. Those that nest in Canada and the northern states migrate south, and some go as far as Mexico for the winter.

EASTERN BLUEBIRD

In the 1930s, an Illinois doctor, alarmed because he no longer saw eastern bluebirds, began to set out nesting boxes in the countryside to encourage their return. After he reported success, scout troops and bird clubs began to follow his example by setting up "bluebird trails"—series of bluebird nesting houses mounted along country roads. Today there are bluebird trails, some with a hundred houses or more, in Canada and in twenty-four states. Many people also put up a box or two near their homes. With this help, eastern bluebirds have made a remarkable recovery.

Male eastern bluebirds are a deep blue above and rusty red on the throat, breast, and sides. The female's colors are similar but not as bright.

37

WESTERN BLUEBIRD

The western bluebird is closely related to the eastern species and similar in its habits. Both hunt by perching on a fence or tree and swooping down upon insect prey. The two look alike except that the western male has a blue throat and a touch of rust color above the wings. The western female is a duller version of her partner.

Like the eastern bluebird, it nests in open country—woodland edges, meadows, and farmlands. Although the western habitat has been less disturbed than the eastern, the population of western bluebirds has also gone down.

Mountain bluebirds nest five thousand feet or more above sea level, in meadows and rangelands with scattered trees and bushes. Their population has also fallen in the past century.

They eat small fruits, as other bluebirds do, but feed mostly on insect food through the entire year. They often locate prey by hovering in the air close to the ground.

The male is entirely blue—sky blue above with lighter underparts. Females are dull gray-brown with a touch of blue in the wings and tail.

MOUNTAIN BLUEBIRD

ATTRACTING BIRDS TO YOUR YARD

Food

Seeds supply the main course at bird feeders in all seasons. Most people begin by offering the mixed seeds sold in bags at supermarkets, hardware stores, and garden shops. The contents of these ready-made mixes vary greatly. Some have large proportions of food that most birds will not eat, such as wheat, milo (sorghum), oats, flax, and buckwheat. You will soon discover what the birds in your yard like by seeing what they leave untouched.

Not all birds have the same tastes, of course, and there can be differences even within a single species. Experience shows that most birds ignore red milo seed. But recent feeding studies have proved that some western species prefer the milo to other common feeds.

Many people abandon ready-made mixes and prefer to mix their own, buying only the seeds their birds prefer. Bags containing a single kind of seed are available in some of the same stores that sell mixed seed and also in bird specialty shops.

Sunflower seed is a favorite of many species. If you have a choice between the large striped sunflower seed and black oil sunflower, buy the latter. It contains more nourishment, and more kinds of birds can handle the thinner shells.

Birds eat the sunflower kernels and drop the hulls on the ground. After a while, you will notice that the ground is bare beneath the feeder. The hulls contain an acid that kills grass. Some people hide the dead grass by putting a bed of wood chips or other mulching material beneath the feeder. You can avoid the mess by serving hulled sunflower seed, but it costs much more.

Millet is a grass seed. Both the white and the red kinds are popular with small birds, although white millet seems to be preferred.

Niger seed, also called thistle seed, is popular with small finches. The seeds are black, very small, and expensive, but because of their size you get a lot of seeds in every pound. Niger should be served in special feeders with tiny openings (see page 42).

Some larger birds like dry whole corn kernels, and small ground-feeders eat cracked corn. All seeds need extra attention in summer because they spoil faster when the weather is hot and wet. This is especially true of cracked corn. Try to put out only as much food as the birds will eat in a day or two. Store seeds in the coolest and driest place you have, and buy quantities that you can use within a few weeks.

Beef suet is attractive to many birds at all seasons. If you decide to offer suet in summer, it too needs special care because it turns rancid in the heat. Some people take the suet in each evening and place it in the freezer overnight. Others put it out only in the cooler hours—morning and late afternoon—and keep it refrigerated the rest of the time.

Peanuts and peanut butter mixtures spoil quickly in hot weather too. There is also some evidence that such high-fat foods cannot be digested by baby birds. It is probably best to avoid using peanut products for most warm-weather feeding.

Hummingbirds and orioles come to special sugar-water feeders (see page 43). Bird specialty stores sell instant mixes, but it's easy to make your own. Here's how:

Ask an adult for help unless you are used to using a stove. Mix one part of sugar into four parts of water in a saucepan and stir to dissolve. Heat the mixture and let it boil for a couple of minutes. Cool before using and store the extra syrup in the refrigerator until you need a refill.

Tanagers, orioles, and some other birds like fruit. You can drive a long nail up through the bottom of a wooden feeder or a piece of wood. Put a piece of orange, apple, melon, pear, banana, or some grapes on the pointed end of the nail. You might also try offering raisins that have been soaked in water to soften them.

In the springtime, when birds are nesting, the females need extra calcium for their eggs. The shells of hens' eggs are a good source of this mineral. You can save the shells, crush them with a rolling pin, and offer them to the birds.

Water

The simplest way to provide water is to put a shallow pan or the cover of a garbage can on the ground and keep it filled. Use a container with sloping sides, if possible. The water should be no deeper than two inches in the middle.

If there is any danger from prowling cats, it is safer to raise the bath above

ground level. Birdbaths on pedestals are sold in garden stores.

Water is most attractive to birds when it is moving. If there are no restrictions on water use where you live, a garden hose can be suspended above the bath and adjusted to allow a very slow drip. Or a plastic jug of water with a tiny hole on its side can be hung from a tree branch above the bath. Holes in the bottom of the jug tend to become plugged up.

A shelf feeder at the window brings the birds close to your view.

Feeders

Different birds have different feeding habits. You will see more kinds of birds in your yard if you feed them on several different levels.

Some birds prefer to feed close to earth. Even if you decide not to scatter food on the ground, some seed will fall from other feeders and end up there.

Most ground-feeding birds also visit any kind of shelf or table. The simplest could be a split log, with the flat side up.

It is fairly easy to make a table feeder from scraps of lumber. Such a feeder, mounted beneath a window or on a patio railing, provides first-class viewing. It should have holes in the floor so rainwater can drain off. Avoid using treated wood, which will contaminate the food.

For safety from cats and better views from the house, a feeder can be mounted on a wooden or metal pole. The feeder should have a roof and drainage holes to keep the food dry. If someone in the house has tools and some skill with them, making a pole feeder can be a home project.

Niger seed is usually served from hanging feeders. These protect the seed from rain and wind and allow the birds to take just one seed at a time. It's a good practice to offer sunflower seed too from a hanging feeder. Some birds will make the hanging feeders their first choice, so there will be less squabbling at other places in the yard where this popular food is offered.

You can make your own hanging feeder by using a ready-made container: a milk carton, a cereal box, or a plastic soda bottle. The carton and box won't last for a long time, but a plastic bottle should be good for a few seasons.

If you decide to buy a feeder, you'll find a wide variety of shapes and materials in the stores. Bird specialty stores usually offer the most choices.

Some plastic feeders break easily when dropped or are soon chewed to pieces by squirrels. The best ones are made of a tough material called polycarbonate and have rust-resistant metal perches and portholes. Plastic has the advantage over wood of being easier to keep clean.

If you buy a wooden feeder, look for one made of a material that resists rot and insect damage, such as cedar or cypress.

Commercial hummingbird feeders are made of plastic or glass. Unless you have hordes of hummers coming to your yard, a feeder holding just a few ounces of syrup is the best choice. Sugar syrup spoils quickly in heat, and the feeders need to be rinsed and refilled often.

Hummingbirds can drink from sugar-water feeders while they hover in midair, but orioles need perches.

You can also make your own, using any kind of narrow container: a test tube or the kind of water bottle sold in pet stores for gerbil cages. Commercial hummingbird feeders are colored red to attract the birds. If you make your own, just tie some red ribbon around it.

Whatever kind of feeder you use, you will want to make sure that birds—not squirrels—get most of the food. To keep squirrels from pole-mounted or hanging feeders, most people use baffles.

Baffles are made of smooth plastic or metal that is curved like a bowl. They are mounted on the pole below the feeder or on the rope that holds a hanging feeder. Plastic baffles are sold in stores that sell feeders. Some people make their own baffles out of a metal garbage can cover, a large can, or a metal bucket. If your feeder is mounted on a pole, you can make a baffle from a two-liter soda bottle. Just cut out the bottom and attach the mouth of the bottle to the pole with a small hose clamp. Squirrels climb the pole, find themselves inside the bottle, and have no place to go but down.

Birds occasionally fly into windows, and some die as a result. If many birds visit your yard, the likelihood of window strikes is greater. Try hanging some strips of ribbon, weighted by small jingle bells, in front of the window that the birds hit. The best solution of all is to cover the outside of the window with the garden netting described in "Backyard

Plants" (see page 46). The threads of the net are so thin that the material doesn't interfere with your view.

Birdhouses and Nesting Shelves

Many people make birdhouses for their yards and mount them on a tree or post. Some birds are fussy and won't use a house that is the wrong size. The following chart contains basic house dimensions for the species discussed in this book and tells how far they should be mounted above ground level.

	Size of Floor	Height of House	Hole Diameter	Height of Hole Above Floor	Distance Above Ground
Bluebirds	5″ x 5″	8″	1½″	6″	4′– 6′
Purple martin*	6″ x 6″	6″	2½″	1″	15′– 20′
Tree swallow	5″ x 5″	6″– 8″	1½″	4″– 6″	10′– 15′
Wrens	4″ x 4″	6″– 8″	1⅛″	4″– 6″	6′– 10′

*Martin houses usually have many units. These are dimensions for a single apartment.

Unlike birdhouses, nesting shelves are open on at least one side. Shelves for barn swallows or eastern phoebes should be six inches high, with a floor measuring six inches by six inches, and mounted eight to twelve feet aboveground.

Use untreated wood for any of these shelters. Floors should have holes for drainage, and boxes need holes in their walls for ventilation. Boxes must have a hinged roof or wall so you can clean them out.

Ready-made houses are sold at many hardware and garden stores and at bird specialty stores. Houses sold for purple martins have many apartments and are usually made of aluminum. These are lighter and much easier to handle than wooden houses, and they are easier to clean.

Houses may attract unexpected guests. Chickadees, titmice, wrens, or nuthatches may use a box meant for bluebirds or martins, and robins or mourning doves use nesting shelves. None of these birds should be disturbed, of course. But if starlings or house sparrows move in, you should clean out their nests as soon as you discover them. You may have to do this several times to discourage the birds.

The books listed on page 47 contain more information about houses. Your local library probably has others giving specific plans for shelters.

Backyard Plants

Since birds depend upon plants for safety and shelter, a bare yard is not very inviting. Birds are more likely to use your feeder if it is near a tree or some bushes, where they can rest between visits. It is even more important to have convenient perches near the birdbath so the birds have a place to preen and dry off after bathing.

Islands of trees, shrubs, and low-growing flowers in any part of the yard will attract birds. If you have a corner where blackberries or other brambles are allowed to grow, this is likely to be a popular spot.

Hummingbirds often come to funnel-shaped blossoms, but they will be drawn to any flower that is rich in nectar. Even if you have no room for a flower garden, you might lure the hummingbirds with some flowers in hanging baskets.

Some of the books listed on page 47 recommend specific plants that provide benefits to bird life.

Insects visit all plants, of course, and almost all birds eat insects. When they do, they also eat any pesticides that were used in the garden. If you attract birds to your yard, you should avoid the use of garden poisons. The birds won't eat all your insect pests, but they will surely reduce their numbers.

Birds can be garden pests too, by eating backyard blueberries, cherries, raspberries, and other fruits before the gardener harvests them. Sometimes the birds pick out vegetable seeds from newly planted beds or tear out seedlings.

The best way to fight fruit damage is to cover the plants with protective garden netting before the fruits ripen. Vegetable seeds and seedlings can be protected with floating row covers made of a lightweight plastic (polypropylene) until the plants are established. These materials are sold in garden stores and through the catalogs of seed suppliers.

Good Housekeeping

Regular cleanup is essential to avoid harming the birds you want to help. Both food and feeders need more attention in warm weather, when molds and bacteria grow quickly.

Uneaten seed and grain should be thrown away after a few days, especially if it has become wet. Try to put out just as much food as the birds will eat in a short time.

Bird droppings, spoiled food, and feathers pile up in feeders. They should be scrubbed out regularly, perhaps once a month.

Hummingbird feeders need more frequent cleaning because mold grows easily in the syrup. Rinse the feeder every two to four days and refill it. Remove any mold with a bottle brush or pipe cleaner. Or pour in some vinegar diluted with water and shake it so the solution reaches all parts of the feeder. Rinse well before refilling.

Birdbaths are easy to clean and refill with a garden hose.

Bird boxes and shelves should be scrubbed out after the young have left the nest.

FOR FURTHER READING

Identifying the Birds

National Geographic Society. *Birds of North America*. Washington, DC: National Geographic Society, 1983.

Peterson, Roger Tory. *A Field Guide to Eastern Birds*. Boston: Houghton Mifflin, 1984.

————. *A Field Guide to Western Birds*. Boston: Houghton Mifflin, 1984.

Robbins, Chandler, Bertel Bruun, Herbert Zim, and Arthur Singer. *Birds of North America*. New York: Golden Press/Western Publishing, 1986.

Attracting the Birds

Burton, Robert. *North American Birdfeeder Handbook*. New York: Dorling Kindersley, 1992.

Dennis, John V. *A Complete Guide to Bird Feeding*. New York: Alfred A. Knopf, 1988.

————. *A Guide to Western Bird Feeding*. Marietta, OH: Bird Watcher's Digest Press, 1991.

————. *Summer Bird Feeding*. Chicago: Prism Creative Group, 1990.

Kress, Stephen W. *The Audubon Society Guide to Attracting Birds*. New York: Scribner's, 1985.

Ortho Books. *Building Birdhouses and Feeders*. San Ramon, CA: Ortho Books, 1990.

There are many more books about feeding and attracting birds. Check the shelves of your local library.

FOR MORE INFORMATION

These nonprofit organizations are dedicated to helping particular bird species:

Purple Martin Conservation Association
Edinboro University of Pennsylvania
Edinboro, PA 16444

North American Bluebird Society
P.O. Box 6295
Silver Spring, MD 20916-6295

INDEX